The Siege of Vicksburg

A Captivating Guide to the Final Battle of Ulysses S. Grant's Vicksburg Campaign during the American Civil War

Free Bonus from Captivating History (Available for a Limited time)

Hi History Lovers!

Now you have a chance to join our exclusive history list so you can get your first history ebook for free as well as discounts and a potential to get more history books for free! Simply visit the link below to join.

Captivatinghistory.com/ebook

Also, make sure to follow us on Facebook, Twitter and Youtube by searching for Captivating History.

Contents

Introduction

The Siege of Vicksburg was debatably one of the most strategically critical events of the American Civil War. The standoff, which lasted from May 18th to July 4th, 1863, was ultimately a Union success, and its conclusion coincided with the Northern victory at Gettysburg, Pennsylvania, on July 3rd. This dual triumph by the federal government was considered the turning point of the Civil War, as the tide of victory began moving in favor of the North. After two years of intense fighting, the Confederacy was finally showing signs of weakening to the delight of President Abraham Lincoln, who received news of both successes on the same afternoon.

The Siege of Vicksburg was part of the more than three-month-long complicated Vicksburg campaign—a daring and unique strategy by Union General Ulysses S. Grant. The Union wanted control of the entire Mississippi River, and Vicksburg was considered the key to gaining the last piece of the waterway that served as a vital supply link to the Southerners. The Vicksburg campaign, which began at the end of March 1863, involved Northern troops penetrating deep into Louisianian enemy territory to circumnavigate the Confederate presence along the Mississippi and circle back east downstream from Vicksburg, crossing the waterways where they were not expected at Bruinsburg. Grant's risk ultimately paid off, but the impenetrable

Vicksburg could not be breached. The only course open was for the Northerners to starve out, dig in, and shell the Confederate Army stationed within the fortress that was Vicksburg.

Forty-seven days later, Confederate General John Pemberton finally relented. His starving men had taken to eating rats, and diseases began to spread rapidly through the squalid conditions of the town. General Grant agreed to a conditional surrender, with the downtrodden Southern troops required to hand in their arms and return home as parolees. Within a week, the final stretch of the Mississippi that was still under Rebel control fell to the Union. Vicksburg remained under Union command for the remainder of the war, and the Southerners' main transport and communication routes through their territories straddling the Mississippi were officially blocked. The Vicksburg campaign was a coup for the Yankees, and it is historically considered the most decisive and influential series of events in the Civil War. The South would never recover.

Chapter 1 – Events Leading to the Vicksburg Campaign

The start of the American Civil War in the spring of 1861 would mark the entire term of President Abraham Lincoln (1809-1865, in off. 1861-1865) as one of domestic warfare. The federal government of the North, which supported the abolition of slavery, fought the Southern slave states, also known as the Confederate States of America (CSA), for four years until the spring of 1865. The Confederates (also referred to as the Rebels or the Southerners) drew the Yankees (also known as the Northerners or Federals) into their territory for most of the war. The Confederacy was formed by eleven states that seceded from the Union of the United States to form their own government. These states—South Carolina, Mississippi, Florida, Alabama, Georgia, Louisiana, Texas, Virginia, Arkansas, Tennessee, and North Carolina—occupied the southeastern extremities of the US. Other regions surrounding the CSA were contested or partly included in the Confederacy during the war, but in 1863, West Virginia split from Virginia to rejoin the Union.

The Vicksburg campaign of 1863 fell within what was known as the Western Theater of the Civil War. This was one of three official theaters, and it included operations in Alabama, Georgia, Florida,

Mississippi, North Carolina, Kentucky, South Carolina, Tennessee, and Louisiana east of the Mississippi River. The Eastern Theater included activities east of the Appalachian Mountains, and those on the west of the Mississippi River fell within the Trans-Mississippi Theater—Missouri, Oklahoma, Arkansas, Kansas, Texas, and Louisiana.

The Union experienced early successes in the war within the Western Theater, mostly due to the command of General Ulysses S. Grant's Army of the Tennessee. Ulysses Grant (1822–1885) had been born Hiram Ulysses Grant but was known to his friends as "Sam." Grant was from Ohio and graduated from West Point Military Academy in New York, along with most of the other commanders who served in the Civil War, whether under the banner of the North or South. However, Grant had a checkered career with the military until the Vicksburg campaign. Grant graduated in 1843 and went on to distinguish himself in the Mexican-American War (1846–1848) but resigned from the army in 1854. Apparently grappling with personal problems that led him to drink, Grant was unsuccessful at the various endeavors he undertook, such as farming, clerking, real estate, and politics. He leaped at the chance to join the Union for the Civil War in 1861, eventually receiving recognition with his twin victories at Forts Henry and Donelson in the Western Theater in February of 1862. His demands for unconditional surrender at Fort Donelson earned him the nickname of "Unconditional Surrender Grant" and led to his promotion to major general. (Grant went on to become the commanding general of the US Army from March 1864 to March 1869.)

Grant's initial failure at the Battle of Shiloh (April 6th-7th, 1862, southwestern Tennessee) forced President Lincoln to replace him with General Henry Halleck (1815–1872, a US army officer, lawyer, and scholar who served two terms with the military and went on to become the commanding general of the US Army). However, Lincoln refused to remove Grant from general command, stating that "I can't spare this man. He fights." Grant was reinstated as a general by July of 1862. He led the Army of the Tennessee and reestablished his reputation through dual victories in northern Mississippi (the Battles of Iuka and Corinth) in September and October of that year. After the end of the Civil War, President Andrew Johnson (1808-1875, in off. 1865-1869) made Grant the general of the US Army, and he also served briefly as the secretary of war before turning to politics as a member of the Republican Party. Grant went on to become the eighteenth president of the United States, serving two terms from 1869 to 1877. As president, he fought hard for justice. He created the Justice Department and worked to protect African Americans during the post-Civil War Reconstruction era.

The mighty Mississippi River that runs north-south, bisecting the US from beyond the Canadian border in the north to the Gulf of Mexico in the south, formed a natural division between the Southern states. Within the areas of fighting during the Civil War, the Mississippi River divided the states of Mississippi, Tennessee, and Kentucky on the eastern bank from Missouri and Arkansas on the western bank. Louisiana, at the far south on the Mexican Gulf, was divided by the river but fell mostly on the west. The Mississippi River provided critical access for naval warfare, the provision of men and supplies, and communications during the Civil War for both Yankees and Rebels alike. Union General William Tecumseh Sherman (1820-1891, American soldier, educator, author, and businessman who played a significant role in the war and who was promoted to major general in May of 1862) stated that the Mississippi was the spine of America. This proved true when the Federals took Vicksburg, thus breaking the backbone of the country.

The critically strategic town of Vicksburg, Mississippi, lay within Southern territory. It was located in Warren County, just south of the conjunction of the Mississippi River and Yazoo tributary, which drained from the northeast. Vicksburg was situated on high bluffs—the Walnut Hills—on the banks of the Mississippi River, overlooking

Louisiana on the western bank. The town was located on a large bend of the Mississippi that circumnavigated the De Soto Peninsula, a part of Louisiana. (In 1876, flooding destroyed this meandering section of the Mississippi to form an oxbow lake—Centennial Lake—and De Soto became an island.)

Vicksburg held a commanding position not only geographically but also as a key Confederate river port during the Civil War, enabling manufactured goods, essential foods from plantations, and soldiers west of the Mississippi to reach the Western and Eastern Theater battlefields east of the mighty waterway. The Southern Railroad ran west-east through Vicksburg, enabling the transfer of these goods from the trans-Mississippi east.

Before the war, Vicksburg's key location in central-west Mississippi adjacent to the river made it a vital hub of trade for the steamboat traffic up and down the river. Large tributaries, such as the Red, Louisiana, and Yazoo Rivers that emptied from the southern states into the Mississippi, carried agricultural goods from far inland to waterfront trading towns. Cotton and other agricultural goods from the surrounding plantations were channeled through the bustling node of Vicksburg. This maritime trade utilized the main arterial route of the Mississippi, which exited into the open ocean of the Gulf of Mexico below New Orleans, Louisiana. The Southerners relied heavily on the ports around the gulf, as well as along the Atlantic seaboard, to transport their goods to the rest of America as well as abroad, particularly to Europe.

The Mississippi was the heart of the economic lifeblood of Southern trade. The North knew this, so one of the North's first strategies of attack at the start of the war in 1861 was to cut off this supply route. The plan had been abandoned in favor of piecemeal land battles, but after two years of fighting, President Lincoln realized that the war would be long and bloody. His attention was then drawn to more strategic approaches, such as controlling Vicksburg. Confederate President Jefferson Finis Davis (1808-1889, a US politician who had served two terms in the US military, served as the American secretary of war for four years, and served the US House of Representatives before joining the Confederacy for the entire Civil War as its) described the town as "the nailhead that holds the South's two halves together." and President Lincoln stated that "Vicksburg is the key! The war can never be brought to a close until that key is in our pocket."

With full knowledge of the importance of the Mississippi River, the Confederacy began fortifying the strategic towns along its banks, especially Vicksburg. The western extent of the town abutted the river, and its bluffs provided the perfect height for artillery batteries to point at the waterfront and riverway. The entire town, like its fellow settlements along much of the eastern bank of the Mississippi, was poised on a series of bluffs forming natural buttresses.

The Confederates further built up the land approaches to the town with earthworks and timber structures. These ramparts were built high, punctured with obstacles such as sharp timbers, and ended in deep ditches—a deathtrap for enemies who managed to get close enough to the fortified town. Batteries of cannons and heavy mortars protected all flanks of the town. The large hairpin bend in the river near Vicksburg forced boats to slow down as they moved past the town, making enemy vessels even more vulnerable to attack. It became increasingly apparent to both the North and South that the place most unlikely to be taken by force was Vicksburg because it was considered virtually impenetrable.

Starting in April of 1862, a series of river and land battles between the North and South saw a myriad of changes with the control points of the Mississippi, from its mouth near New Orleans to beyond Fort Pillow, Tennessee (north of Memphis and 463 kilometers, or 288 miles, upstream from Vicksburg). By the beginning of August 1862, the Union had beaten its way to victory and controlled the entire Mississippi along the battlelines except for a 229-kilometer (142-mile) stretch from Vicksburg downstream to Port Hudson, Louisiana, that became known as the Gibraltar of the South. Land battles in northeastern Mississippi and near Memphis, Tennessee, resulted in Union victories, and by early October of 1862, the time was right for the Federals to march on Vicksburg, as the town was vulnerable to a land attack.

The most likely approach to Vicksburg would have been from the north, northeast, or possibly the east. However, General Ulysses S. Grant was not a conventional man, and he was unlikely to do exactly as the enemy expected. Many senior commanders for both the Yankees and the Rebels had been chosen for leadership in the Civil War due to their particular engineering skills, and these skills would be excessively called upon in the campaign to come.

Chapter 2 – The Vicksburg Campaign

In planning the extraordinarily bold and risky Vicksburg campaign, General Ulysses S. Grant needed to consider the geography and terrain of Vicksburg's situation most seriously. Just north of Vicksburg and east of the Mississippi lay the delta region. This wet and marshy area was prone to flooding and was intersected by numerous streams, bayous, and tributaries to the Mississippi, such as the Yazoo River. Large parts of the delta were virtually impenetrable since the swampland was intersected by many creeks with steep banks and filled with disease-carrying mosquitoes, tangled undergrowth, and deadly beasts and reptiles, such as alligators and snakes.

On the west side of the Mississippi, in Louisiana, the ground was less marshy and flatter, but it would still require extensive corduroying—the laying of pontoons of log walkways across the wider rivers. The potential of heavy rains could turn the existing dirt roads of Mississippi into thick mud or create unexpected flash-flooding. The bluffs upon which Vicksburg was built dissipated northeastward (inland) but were part of a series of bluffs that extended from Columbus, Kentucky, in the north to Baton Rouge, Louisiana, in the south. (This vast stretch along the eastern bank of the Mississippi is more than eight hundred kilometers, or five hundred miles, long.) The bluffs proved to be an ideal natural defensive line for the Confederacy, as the Union had discovered.

General Grant was fortunate to have many good lieutenants under his command, including the controversial but effective Major General Sherman (known as "Cump" to his friends) who led the 15th Corps of the Army of the Tennessee during the Vicksburg campaign. Sherman was subject to severe mental conditions, including deep depression and hallucinations, but his erratic career tended to flourish under the broader command of General Grant, with whom he had an excellent relationship.

The Confederate man appointed to protect Vicksburg was Lieutenant General John Clifford Pemberton (1814-1881), a career army officer who chose to join the Confederacy at the start of the Civil War. Pemberton was placed at the helm of the newly formed Department of Mississippi and East Louisiana and arrived in Jackson on October 9th, 1862, to take charge of the Army of Mississippi. Jackson was about eighty kilometers, or fifty miles, directly east of Vicksburg and the state capital of Mississippi. General Pemberton had not enjoyed a successful career in the Confederate Army until that point, as he proved a better politician than tactician. However, Confederate President Davis had confidence that Pemberton could do better, particularly when placed in the center of the fighting.

Photograph of General Ulysses S. Grant as commander of the Army of the Tennessee for the Federal Army.

Photograph of John C. Pemberton, Lieutenant General of the Confederate Forces of the Army of Mississippi.

Between November of 1862 and March of 1863, the Union engaged in a series of amphibious and land-based attempts to either take Vicksburg or at least distract Pemberton and his approximately thirty-thousand-strong Army of Mississippi away from the prized town. Grant was known to be a master of diversionary tactics. Along with his supporting lieutenants, the Yankees arranged so many sideshow engagements during these five months that when they finally launched the Vicksburg campaign in late March of 1863, Pemberton refused to believe that reports of Grant's tricky maneuvers were possible or true.

In November of 1862, Confederate President Davis had given General Joseph E. Johnston (1807–1891, a career US Army officer who joined the Confederacy for the war and played a considerable part in the war) control of the Department of the West (the Western Theater). Johnston was not pleased about controlling such a large war arena, and he was also ill at ease with his two closest subordinate generals—Pemberton and Bragg.

Major General Braxton Bragg (1817–1876, a career US military officer who joined the Confederacy for the war) commanded the Confederate Army of Tennessee, which would be the last remaining full and functioning Rebel Army after the conclusion of the Siege of Vicksburg. However, both Pemberton and Bragg were required to report directly to Davis at the Confederate headquarters at Richmond, Virginia, and this indirect chain of command would prove problematic, ultimately becoming a major contributing factor to the Southern failure at Vicksburg. Johnston was also denied his request that Confederate forces be concentrated near Vicksburg—a short-sighted decision by the Confederacy that would cost them not only Vicksburg but also ultimately the Civil War. The various leaders of the Confederacy were despondent from the start of the Vicksburg campaign.

In contrast, the Union commanders and troops in the Western Theater were ready and eager for engagement. Some, such as Union General John Alexander McClernand (1812–1900, an American politician and lawyer and Union general in the Civil War), were too enthusiastic. McClernand explicitly wanted an independent command to capture Vicksburg quickly and blamed the entrenched professionalism of seasoned soldiers and their commanders as a major delay in the town's capture. On October 20th, 1862, McClernand received secret orders from the president and the War Office that he could raise a volunteer army to obliterate the "insignificant garrison" defending Vicksburg. But the commanding general of the Union Army, Henry Halleck, was quick in dispatching with McClernand's troops to other areas of fighting around Vicksburg to prevent the ignorant and hasty self-serving plans of the politically ambitious McClernand from being followed through.

McClernand's antics forced General Grant into action, who first began gathering Federal soldiers at the Grand Junction (the intersection of the Mississippi Central Railroad with the Memphis and Charleston Line) in Tennessee. He planned to perform a pincer-like attack with his most trusted commander, General Sherman, deep into Mississippi. Several problems plagued Grant at this point in the war. Besides the threat posed by McClernand, poor intelligence networks, interrupted supplies from the North, and continued resistance from the Confederates hampered the Union plans. However, Grant had been given permission by Halleck to "fight the enemy where you please," and by early December, the Blues (Northerners) had pushed the Grays (Southerners) south of Grenada, north-central Mississippi (225 kilometers, or 140 miles, northeast of Vicksburg). Grant's and Sherman's land pushes had been aided by a Federal force moving east across the Mississippi River from Helena, Arkansas, toward Grenada. (Helena was about 114 kilometers, or 71 miles, south downriver from Memphis, Tennessee.)

General Grant kept Pemberton pinned below Grenada but sent General Sherman back north to Memphis to regroup and prepare for an amphibious attack against Vicksburg. (Memphis was 357 kilometers, or 222 miles, north of Vicksburg.) Grant was concerned about his tenuous supply line as he moved farther into enemy territory. The Confederates under Bragg were performing repeated raids on the Federal supply line, including destroying bridges, supply depots, and stations. Grant's plan at this point was to send Sherman down the Mississippi to land near the river mouth of the Yazoo, where it emptied into the Mississippi just north of Vicksburg. From that point, Sherman was instructed to cut the railroad supply line leading into Vicksburg from the north and begin siege operations.

Sherman moved south down the Mississippi with the promised protection of the Union navy and forty thousand men arranged into four infantry divisions of ten brigades, several batteries including fifty-four guns, and two cavalry (horse-mounted) brigades. But on December 18th, Confederate Major General Earl van Dorn (1820–1863, a career military man who joined the Confederacy for the war) led a cavalry raid with 3,500 horsemen on Grant's main supply depot at Holly Springs. The estimated damage of $1.5 million to Union supplies finally sent Grant retreating back to Memphis, which was eighty kilometers, or about fifty miles, to the northwest.

Sherman landed near Vicksburg in late December and approached the Walnut Hills from the north and northeast, attacking on December 27th. This skirmish was known as the Battle of Chickasaw Bayou. The Confederates had about half the number of men compared to the Union attackers. They were under General Martin Luther Smith (1819–1866, a soldier and civil engineer who joined the Confederacy for the war), but because of the robust fortifications and advantageous high ground, the Rebels managed to fend off the Union. Provisional Confederate divisions under Lieutenant General Stephen Dill Lee (1833–1908, an American soldier and politician who served the Confederacy for the war but no relation to Confederate General-in-Chief Robert E. Lee) and Major General Carter L. Stevenson Jr (1817–1888, a career military man who served the Confederacy for the war) took the major onslaught of the fight. By December 29th, Sherman had withdrawn his troops and placed them on transports to return to Memphis and rejoin General Grant's full Army of the Tennessee. Under Sherman, Colonel John De Courcy's and Major General Francis (Frank) Preston Blair Jr's units had suffered 1,315 casualties in a fruitless assault on Vicksburg, which would by no means be the Yankees' final attempt to storm the town's ramparts.

General Grant continued through the winter of 1862/63 and the spring of 1863 with a multitude of diversionary tactics to both confuse and distract the Confederates. Meanwhile, General John McClernand arrived to take command of Sherman's forces (being senior in rank to Sherman) and led the 13th and 15th Union Corps eighty kilometers (some fifty miles) up the Arkansas River, which is a major tributary to the Mississippi. The mouth of the Arkansas tributary was approximately 209 kilometers (130 miles) south of Memphis and 196 kilometers (122 miles) north of Vicksburg. The Battle of Fort Hindman (also known as the Battle of Arkansas Post) was fought from January 9th to the 11th, 1863, and it resulted in a Union victory and the capture of the fort. Although Union control of Fort Hindman would prevent Confederate naval forays from this point onto the Mississippi River, General Grant was not pleased with McClernand's independent and bold move against the Rebels, and he insisted that Union troops be concentrated to make a full onslaught against Vicksburg.

Federal ironclad gunboats pound Fort Hindman from January 9ᵗʰ to January 11ᵗʰ, 1863. This was a similar scene to that of Union General Porter's attack on Grand Gulf on April 29ᵗʰ, 1863.

https://commons.wikimedia.org/wiki/File:Battle_of_Fort_Hindman.png

After the Union's success on the Arkansas River, Grant undertook plans to divert the Mississippi River away from the shores of Vicksburg. He devised a way to do this by digging a canal along the base of the De Soto Peninsula where it abutted the Mississippi, just north of Vicksburg on the hairpin bend. This attempt at rerouting river traffic away from Vicksburg had been tried and failed by the Union in 1862 because of low water levels and the spread of diseases. Grant failed again in January of 1863 because of high water levels and flooding.

Grant's next ploy was to manipulate Lake Providence, 121 kilometers (75 miles) upriver from Vicksburg on the western Louisiana side of the Mississippi. The Union believed they could access a network of waterways from the lake that would emerge at the Red River, south of Vicksburg. The plan did not work, but the flooding caused by Union engineers would later produce a protective barrier to the right flank of Federal soldiers marching south through Louisiana. The Union continued through the first few months of 1863 with a series of amphibious (mostly digging canals) and land offensive tactics to snatch Vicksburg, but all of them failed. Valuable ships and troops were lost in these efforts.

The Federals also failed to take Fort Pemberton, upriver of the Yazoo River where the Tallahatchie and Yalobusha tributaries joined the Yazoo. During this operation, Union Rear Admiral David Dixon Porter's failed attempt to penetrate Steele's Bayou (just north of Vicksburg) and thus access the Yazoo was aborted when his ships became bogged down in the mud. (Porter, 1813-1891, was a US Navy career admiral from a distinguished naval family.) The Union fleet needed to be rescued by Sherman, who provided protection via land while Porter's boats untangled themselves and then abandoned the mission.

These failed efforts by General Grant at least kept his men fit and busy and simultaneously kept General Pemberton looking over his shoulder, constantly guessing at what Grant would try next. Finally, Grant decided on the most unlikely move of all: to send troops by foot south through Louisiana on the western bank of the Mississippi River. It was an outlandish and risky move, particularly since the Yankees would be marching through enemy territory. However, Grant was decided, and he began sending out decoys to detract from his real intentions. General Grant ordered skirmishes upriver from Vicksburg and raids on Confederate depots away from his main operation.

In the last two weeks of April 1863, Grant sent cavalry raids led by Colonel Benjamin Henry Grierson (1826-1911, a music teacher, businessman, and career army officer who did not like horses after he was kicked and nearly killed by a horse at the age of eight but somehow had a knack at leading cavalry charges) inland through Tennessee and Mississippi. Grant had instructed Grierson to "do all the mischief you can" to detract from the Louisiana march. Grierson, with his 1,700 riders, had an unlikely gift for cavalry raids and made a northeast to southwest dash through the enemy territory surrounding

Vicksburg to distract and baffle the enemy. Grierson covered 965 kilometers (600 miles) during his conquests, which stretched from LaGrange (just south of Memphis) to Baton Rouge (just north of New Orleans). The main purpose of the raids, besides detracting from the Vicksburg campaign, was, of course, to destroy Confederate supply depots and infrastructure and prevent reinforcements from reaching Vicksburg.

To Pemberton, the Yankees seemed to be everywhere at once, and his unreliable intelligence network sent the Confederates scrambling to deal with Grierson. Pemberton was short of cavalry units and was virtually helpless to prevent Grierson's forays. The cavalier Federal colonel managed to capture over three thousand arms stockades, destroy ninety kilometers (fifty to sixty miles) of essential railway and tons of Confederate property, and capture one thousand Southern mules and donkeys that were crucial to the Rebel forces—all within sixteen days. Sherman referred to Grierson's shenanigans as "the most brilliant expedition of the war." Other skirmishes in northeastern Mississippi and northern Alabama, in which both the Northerners and Southerners were victorious, prevented the Rebels from sending further troops and reinforcements toward Pemberton near Vicksburg. The Union commanders were keeping the Confederates' attention well away from Grant's carefully devised plan.

On March 29th, Grant's Army of the Tennessee began the final phase of the Vicksburg campaign and began moving from western Mississippi across the Mississippi River to Louisiana above Vicksburg at Milliken's Bend—about twenty kilometers (twelve miles) upstream from Vicksburg. In Louisiana, they began building bridges and corduroy roads and even filled in swamps in preparation for a torturous 110-kilometer (70-mile) march south, which would take a month. This amphibious plan of attack took the troops deep into enemy territory and through wet and marshy lands replete with deadly reptiles and the potential for sudden flooding. Grant would have his men march inland, away from the Rebel presence, along the western embankments of the Mississippi. The Federals then turned south, marching behind the enemy's backs through Louisiana to a point where they could once again recross the Mississippi at a place controlled by the Union. Once back in southern Mississippi, General Grant intended to make a pounce for Vicksburg from an unexpected direction—the south and the east. A requirement of the plan was to move empty Union gunboats downstream past the batteries at Vicksburg to be used to ferry the Federal troops from the western bank of Louisiana to the eastern bank of Mississippi.

This long, swampy march of the Vicksburg campaign and the movement of forty-two thousand men of the 13th and 17th Corps twice across the Mississippi River would be the largest amphibious military operation in history until the invasion of Normandy during World War II. Grant's tenacious maneuver sent the Yankees heading for the hamlet of Hard Times in Louisiana, located on a horseshoe lake of the river about five kilometers (three miles) west-northwest of Grand Gulf that was safely downriver of the Vicksburg guns. The troops marched on foot through the low ground of the Louisianan backwaters, taking a circuitous route inland away from any enemy presence along the riverbanks.

During the course of the Vicksburg campaign, one Northern newspaper commented that "the army was being ruined in mud-turtle expeditions, under the leadership of a drunkard [Grant], whose confidential adviser [Sherman] was a lunatic!" The ultimate success of a plan as outlandish as the campaign to take Vicksburg proved that perhaps the eccentricities of these leaders were an asset at the time. (In fact, Sherman had initially urged against Grant's unorthodox plans, but he eventually capitulated.)

Simultaneous to the Army of the Tennessee's hustle through enemy territory, the Union needed to open up a strategic node on the eastern bank of the Mississippi River to which the troops could be ferried. The fortified town of Grand Gulf—fifty-three kilometers, or thirty-three miles, south of Vicksburg—was chosen as the rendezvous point. Confederate Brigadier General John Stevens Bowen (1830–1863, a career US Army officer who joined the Confederacy) was in command of Grand Gulf, and he had been warning Pemberton of Union activity across the river in Louisiana. However, Pemberton had dismissed such notions as improbable rumors. Confederate General Pemberton was so confident that Grant had given up the fight for Vicksburg that he offered to send a contingent of his men from the Army of Mississippi located at Vicksburg to Major General Bragg's Army of Tennessee. It was only in mid-April that General Pemberton received hard intelligence that the Federals were indeed making a circuitous move through the trans-Mississippi, and by April 17th, there could be no doubt of the enemy's intentions.

During the dark, moonless night of April 16th, Rear Admiral Porter took the opportunity to move empty Union gunboats past Vicksburg south downriver to be used later as transports for the soldiers to recross the river. Porter successfully moved seven ironclad gunships, one armed ram, three army transport vessels, and a tugboat under the noses of the Rebels. Porter's ships ran the gauntlet past Vicksburg under heavy fire, and although many of the boats were somewhat damaged by Confederate artillery positioned on the bluffs, the Union vessels made it safely past. (Only 68 of the 525 rounds fired found a target.)

Porter sailed as close to the waterfront as possible, with the idea being that the long-range guns would fire over their heads. The Union gunboats extinguished their own lights and were additionally protected by coal barges lashed at the side that faced the Rebel batteries, as well as being packed with piles of straw, cotton, and grain to take the major impact of the shelling. Porter lost only one transport of his fleet during his daring midnight dash. The ladies who came out in Vicksburg to watch the passing of Porter reportedly created an ethereal scene, as their full white dresses were illuminated by the Confederate bonfires, cannon blasts, and smoke. (The citizens of Vicksburg had been celebrating with a grand ball on the same night due to the alleged withdrawal of the Yankees from their territory!)

On April 22nd, a second Union flotilla ran the gauntlet, again losing just one vessel but with no loss of life. This time, five of six vessels made it downstream, and, most importantly, so did 600,000 rations. (The sixth damaged vessel floated downstream with its crew, unharmed.) General Grant's audacious plan of attack now became paramount. It would be impossible to move Porter's naval contingent on the slow route back upstream and against the Mississippi current unharmed, as they would become fodder for the Vicksburg bluff batteries.

On April 29th, Admiral Porter's gunboats bombarded Grand Gulf for six hours but failed to take the stronghold, which, similar to Vicksburg, was built on high, easily defendable bluffs. The Yankee vessels were significantly damaged by heavy fire from eight heavy cannons under Bowen's command. The Union suffered seventy-five casualties, while the Confederates only had twenty-two. The smaller settlement of Bruinsburg, about fifteen kilometers (nine miles) south of Grand Gulf, was identified as a replacement landing point. Bruinsburg was nineteen kilometers (twelve miles) from Port Gibson, a small inland town that would provide an ideal staging point for the Union Army.

Sherman simultaneously created a ruckus at Snyder's Bluff north of Vicksburg to distract Pemberton. On April 29th and May 1st, Sherman engaged against the Confederates in what was essentially a Union feint, and he was easily repulsed. Snyder's Bluff was twenty kilometers (twelve miles) northeast of Vicksburg, alongside the Yazoo tributary and built upon an extension of the bluffs of Vicksburg. A Union captain named John Cheney who was stationed at Snyder's Bluff included the following passage in a letter home to his wife, describing the terrain in which the campaign was conducted:

"We are about 8 miles from V [Vicksburg], and can see it through our glasses...The Bluffs are very high, and the country very rough and heavy timbered...the weather is very hot indeed...The Yazoo is inhabited principally by Crockodiles [sic] which may be seen at any time."

On April 30th, Union gunboats began ferrying seventeen thousand troops across the Mississippi from Disharoon's plantation in Louisiana to Bruinsburg, Mississippi. The Federal troops had moved south from Hard Times to be able to cross the Mississippi River at Bruinsburg, which was too insignificant to put up resistance. By the late afternoon on that same day, the 13th Corps had been unloaded in Bruinsburg and begun the march east along the road to Port Gibson. Bayou Pierre was a river that lay north of Port Gibson, running northeast to southwest toward its mouth on the Mississippi at Bruinsburg. Bayou Pierre separated Port Gibson from the desired battleground to the north, as well as Vicksburg. General McClernand hurried his troops onward toward Port Gibson, worrying that the Confederates could destroy the bridges across Bayou Pierre since they must by now surely know of the Yankee plans.

Chapter 3 – The Race for Vicksburg

The Big Black River tributary of the Mississippi that emptied at Grand Gulf lay north of Bayou Pierre, stretching northeast past Vicksburg (south of the town). The Big Black and Bayou Pierre would serve as the main battlelines across which the Northerners made a push for Vicksburg, which took place from the beginning of May to mid-May 1863. When Federal troops began marching from Bruinsburg Landing on April 30th, their commander diverted them off the main road leading to Port Gibson and onto a subsidiary road running parallel to it that joined Rodney Landing (south of Bruinsburg on the Mississippi and Admiral Porter's alternative landing site before he was informed of Bruinsburg by an escaped slave) to Port Gibson. McClernand was sure that the Confederates must be aware of the Northerners' movements and plans, and he expected obstructions along the main route since the Rebels would have set up defenses to prevent the Northern march on Vicksburg.

The terrain around Port Gibson was treacherous, as it was full of steep ravines and high ridges, making it a poor and dangerous potential battleground. Besides the terrain, night was falling, and McClernand wanted to avoid trouble for the time being. Meanwhile, at Bruinsburg, a further twenty-five thousand Federal troops were being delivered at Bruinsburg after having made the Mississippi crossing. These soldiers of General McPherson's 17th Corps under Major General John Alexander Logan (1826-1886, an American soldier and politician) provided a protective backstop to the 13th, which was moving ahead.

Confederate General Bowen, located at Grand Gulf, was by now well aware of the enemy's plans, and he called to Pemberton at Vicksburg for reinforcements. With the growing presence of abundant Yankee troops to his south, the most likely outcome for the Confederates would be to abandon Grand Gulf entirely in order to move outward and fight.

And as the Union columns marched up the Rodney-Port Gibson road, two Southern units were ready for them. Bowen had dispatched Brigadier General Martin E. Green's detachment to establish roadblocks west of Port Gibson. (Green, 1815-1863, was a politician, judge, and commander for the Confederacy, and he was killed by a Federal sharpshooter on June 27th during the Siege of Vicksburg.) Green's force was placed on the Rodney Road near Magnolia Church. A freshly arrived Alabama brigade dispatched from Vicksburg under Brigadier General Edward Tracy (1833-1863, a lawyer who joined the Confederacy for the war but was killed during the Battle of Port Gibson the next day by a Union sharpshooter) searched the road to Bruinsburg for the invaders. Backup brigades from Vicksburg—Brigadier General William Edwin Baldwin's Louisiana and Mississippi troops—hurried from Vicksburg to join the potential fight. Other Confederate units were dispatched from Vicksburg but would not arrive in time.

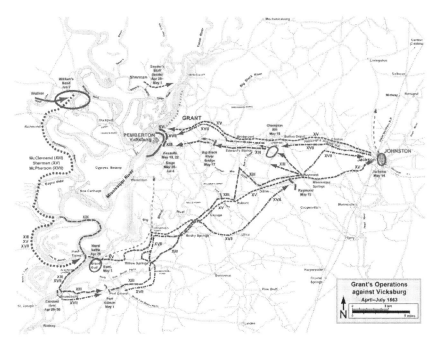

Union operations against the Confederacy in central Mississippi during the Vicksburg campaign from April to July 1863. (Blue for Northerners, red for Southerners.)

Map by Hal Jespersen, https://www.cwmaps.com/, CC BY 3.0
<https://creativecommons.org/licenses/by/3.0>, via Wikimedia Commons
https://commons.wikimedia.org/wiki/File:VicksburgCampaignAprilJuly63.png

As April 30th ticked into May 1st, a Federal column near Magnolia Church finally connected with General Green's men, and the Battle of Port Gibson began—one of the few engagements of the Civil War to occur partially at night. The Union men under Brevet Major General Eugene Asa Carr (1830-1910, a career military man who was awarded the Medal of Honor during the Civil War) engaged in artillery fire from the ravines west of Port Gibson, but the commander ultimately called off the fight, as it proved futile in the darkness.

The Battle of Port Gibson continued during the day from 8:30 a.m. to 5 p.m. on Friday, May 1st, as the vastly outnumbered Confederates attempted to prevent the Union from taking Port Gibson and Grand Gulf. The first movement at Port Gibson was Union Major General Peter Joseph Osterhaus's division moving north to meet Tracy's Alabamian regiment on the Federal's left flank.

(Osterhaus, 1823–1917, was a German-American military man and diplomat.) At this point, Tracy's and Green's wings were widely separated, with Tracy's men fighting just south of Bayou Pierre and Green's men battling farther south near Magnolia Church. The Confederates started the day with a mere 2,500 men on the field.

When Tracy was killed, Colonel Isham Warren Garrott (1816–1863, who was killed on June 17th during the campaign by a Union sharpshooter just after his promotion to brigadier general) took command. Even though there was confusion over leadership, the Confederates managed to hold off the Union troops until late in the afternoon due to their advantageous tactical position on the tricky terrain. Around Magnolia Church, the Rebels under Green fought Brigadier Generals Carr and Alvin Peterson Hovey's (1821–1891, a politician, jurist, and military officer) divisions, ultimately forcing Green and his outnumbered men to retreat behind Center's Creek in alignment with the remaining Rebel Army. (Center's Creek ran north-south just west of Port Gibson, joining Bayou Pierre to the Rodney Road.)

As Green's troops joined to reinforce Garrott, Federal reinforcements under Logan's 17th were moved from Bruinsburg, along with General Grant, to face off against the Confederate grouping. These Union forces pushed the Rebels northeast. On a second front, east of Magnolia Church, McClernand and his divisions (including Carr and Hovey) had taken up the fight against Brigadier Generals Baldwin and Francis Marion Cockrell's divisions. (Baldwin, 1827–1864, was a bookstore owner and militia member who joined the Confederacy for the Civil War; Cockrell, 1834–1915, was a politician who served the Confederacy.) Cockrell's men included the Missouri Brigade, which had been released last and in haste from Grand Gulf where Bowen had held them in the event that further Federals would attempt a crossing. (General Bowen had not been sure until the last moment that most of the Army of the Tennessee was crossing just below his fortification of Grand Gulf.) Despite the Rebel additions to the Battle of Port Gibson, by the late afternoon, considerable Union surges forced the Rebels to retreat, particularly since daylight would soon begin fading. Overall, Bowen's men had been outnumbered three to one and had inflicted 875 casualties on the enemy but only suffered 787 themselves.

Although the Rebels fought valiantly, they eventually retreated north and east behind Bayou Pierre and then the Big Black River, leaving Grand Gulf open to the Federals. Despite losing the battle, Brigadier General Bowen had managed to delay the encroachment of the enemy for a day and had personally led two counterattacks at the Battle of Port Gibson. For this, he was promoted to major general later that month on May 25th, although this promotion was never ultimately approved by the Confederate Congress. Later, at the Battle of Champion Hill, Bowen led a counterattack that almost split Grant's army in two, but since reinforcements from Pemberton and Johnston failed to materialize, the Federals were eventually able to advance on Vicksburg.

After the Battle of Port Gibson, General Grant decided to head north toward the strategic Southern Railroad that linked Vicksburg to Jackson. He made feints toward the Big Black River en route to confuse the enemy, who was backed up between the Big Black and Vicksburg, remaining on the defensive. Grant marched with the combined corps of McClernand's 13th and General James Birdseye McPherson's 17th. McPherson (1828–1864) was a career US army officer, and he was killed the following year in the Battle of Atlanta; he was the second-highest-ranking Union officer killed in the Civil War. Sherman's 15th Corps was moving south from Snyder's Bluff overland, and when the Union army reunited, Grant would have a force forty-five thousand men strong, being supplied by wagons from a beachhead at Grand Gulf.

Confederate General Pemberton had called on two commanders: Major General William Wing Loring (1818-1886, a career military officer who served the US, the Confederacy, and then in Egypt), who took charge of the Confederates on the bluffs behind the Big Black River, and Brigadier General John Gregg (1828-1864, a Texan politician who served the Confederacy but was killed in 1864 during the Siege of Pittsburg). Gregg rode from Port Hudson with three thousand men toward Raymond. The town of Raymond formed the southern point of a triangle, with the town of Edwards nineteen kilometers (twelve miles) to the northwest and Jackson twenty-six kilometers (sixteen miles) to the northeast. (Edwards was twenty-seven kilometers, or seventeen miles, east of Vicksburg and about ten kilometers, or six miles, east of the Big Black River.)

The Battle of Raymond ensued on May 12th when Gregg's force stationed near the town were confronted with Federals they believed to be merely a contingent of the far wing of the Union Army marching north. Gregg believed that Grant was making a western feint toward the Southern Railroad near Edwards when, in fact, Gregg was facing the vanguard of McPherson's entire 17th Corps—the right wing of the full Union Army. Pemberton, assuming that Grant was marching on Jackson and that Gregg was in contact with Grant's rear troops, ordered Gregg to attack. This instruction was a mistake, and by the time Gregg realized he was facing the full might of the Army of the Tennessee, his tiny force of no more than four thousand men was heavily outnumbered. They engaged with the enemy along Fourteen Mile Creek.

After a few hours of fighting, from noon until 2:30 p.m., Gregg withdrew his troops toward Jackson. At Jackson, the main Confederate force had been gathering under General Johnston in anticipation of the Union's move toward Vicksburg. The unfortunate skirmish at Raymond prevented Gregg from joining Pemberton at Vicksburg and also convinced Union General Grant to march on Jackson and flush out the entire Confederate force. Grant had originally been heading northwest toward the Big Black River and on toward Vicksburg, but the thought of approaching Vicksburg with Johnston's army at his rear (to the east, in Jackson) resulted in a change of tactic. The Battle of Raymond had resulted in 515 Confederate and 446 Federal casualties.

The next day, on Wednesday, May 13th, McPherson's and Sherman's troops began moving toward Jackson. McPherson was to go via the settlement of Clinton, which was just west of Jackson. McClernand's 13th was required to remain near Raymond to protect the Union rear from Pemberton as they marched on the Mississippi capital of Jackson. Confederate General Johnston arrived at Jackson on the same day, and realizing the town was not prepared to fend off the Yankees, he ordered an immediate evacuation. His words, "I am too late," proffered a defeatist attitude since Confederate reinforcements moving toward Jackson could have held off the enemy, allowing time for Pemberton to attack from the west and thus protect Vicksburg.

General Johnston was in Mississippi against his will, having been instructed to move his men by President Davis. Johnston's reticence at partaking in the Vicksburg campaign would signal a Confederate failure at this time in the western arena of the war, leading to the loss of Vicksburg and ultimately control of the Mississippi. The inability of Confederate Generals Pemberton and Johnston to work together and go on the offensive to each other's and to General Bowen's aid led to their inevitable failure.

The army and civilians of Jackson decamped to Canton, just northeast of Jackson. On May 14th, the Union began shelling the town, meeting with General Gregg's unit that had remained to hold the city until vital records and other paraphernalia were removed. A heavy thunderstorm in the morning prevented the Union from making a full assault, as roads turned to mud and artillery became problematic to move forward. Later that day, when the weather cleared, Sherman moved in from the south to find abandoned trenches. McPherson, who was approaching from the west, was able to capture the last remaining Confederates, those sacrificial lambs left to put up a fight during the Rebel withdrawal. The Battle of Jackson on May 14th was the first of two in the Vicksburg campaign, with the second ensuing after the end of the Siege of Vicksburg, which essentially closed off the campaign altogether. Unfortunately, this rather fruitless battle on a rainy day in May resulted in three hundred casualties for the Confederates and an estimated nine hundred for the Union.

However, General Grant had achieved his objective, as he had split the Southern Army and removed Johnston, for the time being, from the field. Grant turned his attention west to the enemy lying behind the Big Black River—his only obstacle in capturing Vicksburg. During the Battle of Jackson, Johnston had called for aid from Pemberton to attack the Yankees at Clinton, but Pemberton had hesitated. He did not want to leave Vicksburg vulnerable, and he was also aware that McClernand's troops would block any eastern advance along the Raymond-Edwards road. Pemberton ultimately made a half-hearted decision to move out from Vicksburg, leaving two divisions to defend the town, but he moved southeast, cutting off the Union supply line instead of making a full-frontal attack where he knew the enemy would be ready and waiting.

Departing Vicksburg on May 15th, Pemberton and his three divisions under Generals Loring, Bowen, and Stevenson made poor progress since Baker's Creek on the east of Edwards was flooded. General Pemberton was unaware that Jackson had been abandoned and that Sherman's troops were in the process of laying waste to the capital's government buildings, supply depots, and railroads. Having made little advancement that day, Loring's men camped just east of Baker's Creek at the vanguard of Pemberton's army. Bowen's and Stevenson's men formed a line northwest behind Loring.

Early on the morning of Saturday, May 16th, Pemberton finally received word from Johnston that Jackson had been lost to the Federals and that he must march his troops toward Clinton. As the Confederates began moving north, they clashed unexpectedly with McClernand's corps on the Raymond-Edwards road, as well as a middle road closer to the Jackson-Edwards road. Having not sent out advanced cavalry, Pemberton arranged his men in three defensive divisions along the Jackson Creek ridge for a stretch of approximately five kilometers (three miles). Jackson Creek ran parallel to Baker's Creek in a northeast-southwesterly direction just south of the Southern Railroad. Champion Hill was on the Jackson-Edwards road just to the west of Baker's Creek and north of the intersection with the middle road.

The battle that unfolded on May 16th is known as the Battle of Champion Hill or the Battle of Baker's Creek. The battle continued on two fronts, similar to the Battle of Port Gibson. Confederate General Stevenson and his commanders took on Union Generals Logan's, Hovey's, Carr's, and Osterhaus's units around Champion Hill—McPherson's corps on the Union's right wing. Confederate Generals Bowen and Loring fought a little farther south along the Jackson-Raymond road against Union Major General Andrew Jackson Smith (1815–1897, a career military man) and his units under a division of the 13th corps, with Major General Frank Blair's unit in support of Smith—McClernand's corps or the left wing.

The Blues and Grays fired at one another on a hot spring day in an exhausting series of charges and countercharges. By 1:00 p.m., Pemberton's far left flank was weakening, and as the Federals pushed back, the Rebel line was in danger of collapsing the entire army. Poor working relationships between the Confederate commanders meant that Generals Seth Maxwell Barton (1829–1900, a career military man who served the Confederacy for the war and went on to become a chemist) and Stephen D. Lee were not reinforced against McPherson's onslaught. Bowen finally rushed northeast, battering his way with Cockrell's Missourians onto the "Hill of Death" or Champion Hill, thus severely unsettling the Union and threatening their right wing. But the Blues had several reserve units to muster toward the fight, and Bowen's men found themselves isolated and unsupported upon the hill, with Bowen reportedly holding a magnolia flower in one hand and a sword in the other. Loring, however, had purposefully refused Pemberton's order to move forward to hold Champion Hill and the Rebels' left wing. Loring cited the presence of McClernand's forces as his reason for holding his ground, which was a seemingly futile excuse because McClernand never really seemed to engage in the battle that day at all, something that was particularly noted by General Grant.

Bowen was forced to retreat from Champion Hill, and this move signaled the final push by the Union, whose numbers simply overwhelmed the enemy, pushing them back toward Baker's Creek. Pemberton ordered an official retreat to be led by Bowen and Stevenson, with Loring holding the field to protect the withdrawing columns. The rearguard brigade assigned to hold off the enemy included a friend of Pemberton's, Brigadier General Lloyd Tilghman (1816-1863, an engineer and military man who had served the US Army before joining the Confederacy), who was killed by artillery fire. A clear path back to Vicksburg for the Confederates was blocked by the Federals, and the Rebels needed to divert slightly south toward the Raymond Road in order to get behind the safety of the Big Black River. Loring was so concerned that the Union divisions under Carr would block his exit route that he eventually led his troops south and then northeast to join with Johnston's forces, thus removing Loring's reinforcements from the final race to Vicksburg.

By late afternoon, Grant's men had taken Baker's Creek Bridge, and by midnight on the 16th, they controlled Edwards. In the early hours of Sunday, May 17th, Grant sent McPherson and Sherman north over the Southern Railroad to block the Confederate retreat to Vicksburg. McClernand was instructed to approach the enemy head-on at the intersection of the Big Black River and the railroad where they had camped for the night.

A temporarily constructed pontoon bridge over the Big Black River that was built for Union General Sherman's men to cross on their way to Vicksburg, May 17th, 1863.

https://commons.wikimedia.org/wiki/File:Pontoon-bridge-big-black-river-1863.jpg

The exhausted and dejected Confederate troops in Bowen's corps had disadvantageously camped on the eastern side of the Big Black as they awaited Loring's division that was, by then, marching east toward General Johnston. This delay by Pemberton would prove fatal. The Union under Brigadier General Michael Kelly Lawler (1814–1882, an Irish-born American who served two terms in the Civil War and was a lawyer and farmer by trade), a unit of General Carr's divisions, struck first at the enemy's left wing in the Battle of Big Black River (or the Battle of Black River Bridge) on Sunday morning. The Confederates proceeded with a panicky retreat across the river, and a Missourian observed that many "either swam the river, were captured or killed in trying to get over."

The Rebels managed to defend themselves by using artillery on the bluffs along the western bank of the Big Black River. These defenses provided sufficient time for most of Pemberton's men to escape, but the fatalities in Bowen's division, particularly along the left flank, were high, while the Union suffered few casualties that day. The battle was a rout that sent the Confederates scurrying toward Vicksburg, burning bridges as they retreated to delay the advancing Union.

One thousand eight hundred Confederate soldiers were captured near the Big Black as they hurried to cross two bridges near their encampments west toward Vicksburg. General Pemberton was once again acting contrary to Johnston's direct orders to escape to the northeast toward the remainder of the Confederate Army near Canton. Johnston was rightly concerned that Pemberton's army would be trapped at Vicksburg and ultimately be lost to the Union, which is precisely what happened. Pemberton reached Vicksburg in time to continue his dogged determination to defend the town at all costs by May 17th, but he was hotly pursued by the Federals. The utterly defeated ragtag Army of Mississippi still managed to establish bandstands on the town's hills, where they played the Southern tunes of "Dixie" and "Bonnie Blue Flag" and beat drums to encourage their men.

The Battle of Champion Hill had seen twenty-three thousand Confederate forces face thirty-two thousand Union men since Sherman's corps had arrived too late to join the fight. Confederate losses were 3,800, while Grant recorded 2,400 casualties. The entirety of Grant's Vicksburg campaign had resulted in a set of cascading events in his favor. After the blood-soaked day of Champion Hill, Vicksburg was almost entirely vulnerable to the Union approach. Had Grant lost the day, his supply lines into enemy territory would have been cut off and his army pressured from Pemberton to the west and Johnston to the east. It could have been inevitable that Grant would lose his Army of the Tennessee. But the victory of Baker's Creek (Champion Hill) and the removal of Loring's men from Grant's intended westward march had demoralized and weakened the Rebels standing between him and Vicksburg. Pemberton and Johnston's inability to work together would further muster Grant's cause. When Grant won Champion Hill, then overran the Big Black River, he won Vicksburg. When the Union won Vicksburg, they won the

Mississippi. And once the Yankees had the Mississippi, it was simply a matter of time before they won the Civil War.

Chapter 4 – The Siege of Vicksburg

When Confederate General Pemberton and his commanders and men reached Vicksburg, he immediately began arranging his approximately thirty-thousand-strong force into four divisions to defend the town. General Martin Smith was positioned at the north end, or left flank, of the town. Major General Carter Stevenson was at the south, or right flank, of the defensive line, and Major General John Horace Forney's men held the east of Vicksburg, or the central flank. Bowen's division, just having fled the field, was kept in reserve, although they would ultimately serve the center. Smith's and Forney's men were the fresh reserve divisions that had been withheld at Vicksburg by Pemberton.

Grant marched his troops toward Vicksburg, disappointed he hadn't bagged the enemy before they settled into their considerable entrenchments. Having come upon the fortified town by Monday, May 18th, and after taking time to repair the bridges destroyed by the withdrawing Southerners, the Union soldiers arranged themselves to make a charge for the town in anticipation of bombarding the Rebels before they had time to arrange themselves. At this stage, the Blues had approximately thirty-five thousand men available for battle, but as the fight for Vicksburg raged on into early July, the Union numbers would swell to over seventy thousand men, as reinforcements were added to their original number, including the reserve 9th Corps under Major General John Parke and the 16th Corps, a detachment under Major General Cadwallader C. Washburn. The Yazoo River was now available to the Federals to ship in fresh men as well as rations and supplies to keep Vicksburg surrounded.

General Pemberton had lost approximately half his men in the battles of the preceding two weeks, and considering the addition of Admiral Porter's naval units manning the Mississippi, the Confederates became hopelessly outnumbered and entirely surrounded by the Yankees. When the Federals first arrived on the scene, Pemberton had approximately half their number—18,500 able men—to defend Vicksburg since the remainder of his army needed to recover from the prelude to the siege. But the topography upon which Vicksburg was situated and the earthwork and fortification preparations along the ten-kilometer (six-and-a-half-mile) defensive line of the land approach had made it a fortress.

To the north, Fort Hill perched on a high bluff overlooking the great bend in the Mississippi. To the northeast, its neighbor, the highly elevated Stockade Redan, an arrow-shaped timber fortification of the embankment, boasted an impregnable approach along the Graveyard Road. Next, two redans, including the 3rd Louisiana, led on to the Great Redoubt, a four-sided square fortification that protected the road east from Jackson. Just south of the town, the 2nd Texas Lunette, a four-sided pointed fortification, covered the Baldwin's Ferry Road leading southeast into Mississippi, and just south of the lunette, the Railroad Redoubt protected the Southern Railroad exit. Square Fort (Fort Garrott) was situated at the southeastern extremity of the town's fortifications on the Hall's Ferry Road, and finally, South Fort abutted the Mississippi at the southern point of the perimeter.

At first, Sherman's 15th held the northern bluffs (Hayne's Bluff), or the right flank of the Union, adjacent McPherson's 17th Corps at the northeast surrounding the Jackson Road, covering the central-right flank. McClernand's 13th was positioned southeast of Vicksburg, manning the left Union flank around the Baldwin's Ferry Road and the Southern Railroad. The first Union attack on May 19th was from the north under General Sherman's corps, and it was led by Major General Frank Blair Jr, followed later by an impressive charge by Major General Hugh Boyle Ewing's brigade. (Ewing, 1826–1905, was a diplomat, attorney, author, and foster brother of General Sherman.) The Bluecoats charged down the northbound Graveyard Road toward the Rebels' formidable timber enforced Stockade Redan. They not only had to negotiate a treacherous ravine on the approach but also faced an impressive assortment of abatis—rows of sharp timbers pointed outward.

Along the north and northeast defense line, Smith's, Cockrell's, and Bowen's men pounded the Northerners with artillery and musket fire from their ramparts five meters (seventeen feet) above. When the enemy came as close as the deep ditches below the ramparts (the First Battalion of the 13th against the Confederate 36th Mississippi), they could do nothing but crouch in the 1.8-meter (6-foot) deep and 2.5-meter (8-foot) wide furrows. The Rebels above were forced to improvise by rolling and hurling fused six- and twelve-pound cannonballs down the slopes, as they were unable to discharge artillery at such close range. The Yankees made no real progress that day, and McPherson's and McClernand's men did not engage sufficiently to warrant any Yankee success. Federal losses (killed, wounded, and missing) for the day were a thousand men to the Confederates' two hundred casualties.

General Grant did not intend to engage in a long siege, and his relentless approach led him to attack the town a few days later. On May 22nd, Grant tried his luck again, sending his three main corps in a full assault against Vicksburg at about 10 a.m. after four hours of futile artillery bombardment from the land and river. The Federals approached across an intimidating five-kilometer (three-mile) front, equipped with ladders to scale the embankments, which would ultimately prove too short to do the job! At the north, Sherman was once again repulsed at Stockade Redan. McPherson's troops, which were approaching down the Jackson Road, recoiled under heavy Confederate fire after marching against the 3rd Louisiana Redan and the pivotal eastern Great Redoubt. McPherson suffered particularly heavy losses at the Great Redoubt. Only McClernand's units were successful in breaching the Southern barrier that day. The Yankees pushed through, overcoming the 2nd Texas Lunette on the Union's left flank. Further brigades under McClernand forced the Railroad Redoubt to be evacuated and put severe pressure on South Fort and Square Fort.

But McClernand needed assistance from Sherman and McPherson to persevere with his breakthroughs, and help was not forthcoming in time. Grant's open prejudice toward McClernand undermined the commanding general's belief that his subordinate had, in fact, made progress. Although a small contingent from McPherson's corps eventually helped, McClernand's troops were forced back by the Texans under General Stevenson, as well as Confederate General Green's division, in the late afternoon. The Rebels retook their forts and redoubts and flushed the Yankees from the field. McClernand's boasting to the press and his troops about his conquests led to his early and unfair dismissal on June 18th from the field of battle at Vicksburg, but it did not end his career.

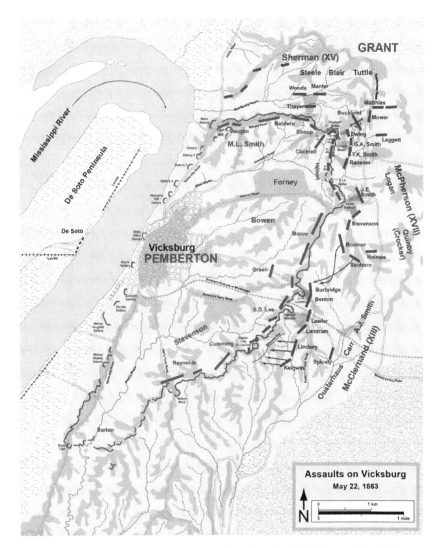

Arrangement of troops for the Union's second push against Vicksburg on May 22nd, 1863. This was a similar arrangement to the troop positions on May 19th. (Blue for Northerners, red for Southerners.)

Map by Hal Jespersen, https://www.posix.com/CW/, CC BY 3.0 <https://creativecommons.org/licenses/by/3.0>, via Wikimedia Commons https://commons.wikimedia.org/wiki/File:VicksburgMay22.png

General Grant's incomplete attack had cost him 3,200 men (killed, wounded, and missing), while the defenders of Vicksburg had lost less than 500. It was then that Grant decided to lay siege to the town rather than conduct further futile offensives. His field surgeons had convinced him that diseases amongst his men (similar to those afflicting the Confederates within the town), as well as the wounded in the field, needed attention. By May 25th, Grant agreed not to conduct further direct attacks on Vicksburg for the time being, but the stalwart general did not agree to a withdrawal. (On this day, a general ceasefire was called, during which the dead and wounded from both sides were retrieved, with the surviving soldiers intermingling as if nothing was amiss.)

Grant intended to set up a permanent camp to entrap the enemy in order to avoid as many causalities as possible. The Union general extended his siege line to twenty kilometers (twelve miles) around Vicksburg. Heavy siege mortar fire and shelling would continue from a distance, which was followed by random musket fire that eventually became a kind of game for the adversaries, as they fired across the battle lines at both fake and real targets. Finally, the lethal work of sharpshooters became the most strategic tactic, as the Blues and Grays positioned snipers to take out unfortunates whose heads rose too high above the parapets and ditches as they worked. The siege would last for six weeks, with devastating consequences for the Rebels.

The Federal move south through Mississippi during 1862 and the first half of 1863 had seen mass evacuations of civilians from those areas, as buggies laden with delicate, panicked ladies, their household possessions, and black slaves fled for safer areas as the Yankees drew toward them. Approximately half the citizens of Vicksburg had fled in the seventeen-day run-up to the Siege of Vicksburg, which had seen five overland engagements across their stretch of Mississippi and five Union victories.

The siege during the sweltering summer of 1863 made the remaining residents of Vicksburg and their slaves literally dig in to protect themselves from the almost continual bombardment of Minié balls (large bullets), Parrott shells, and further barrage. The Union continued firing on the town throughout the days, pausing only for meals. On land, the Northerners surrounded the town in a semicircle that covered the northern, eastern, and southern flanks of the town. From the west, Rear Admiral Porter's gunboats fired on Vicksburg from the Mississippi, and his naval convoy continued to supply the Union with food and supplies. The residents of Vicksburg were forced to live in natural caves in the bluffs or in hurriedly constructed dugouts within the ground in shanty-style burrows. When the Civil War began in 1861, Vicksburg had a population of approximately 4,500 people—one of the largest towns in Mississippi—but at the time of the siege, this had diminished to approximately 2,000 civilians. The family plantation of President Davis, Brierfield, was a short fifty-three kilometers (thirty-three miles) south of Vicksburg.

May 29th was a particularly brutal day of shelling, although it was just one of many that lived on in the memories of Vicksburg's citizens. The Union bombardments destroyed buildings and homes, killing civilians and soldiers in the process, including children asleep in their makeshift beds within the caves. Domestic homes temporarily being used as field hospitals were likewise hit, killing or further injuring the sick and wounded within. During the shelling, the citizens took to their cellars, shelters, and caves, but they emerged in the quiet periods to carry on life as usual.

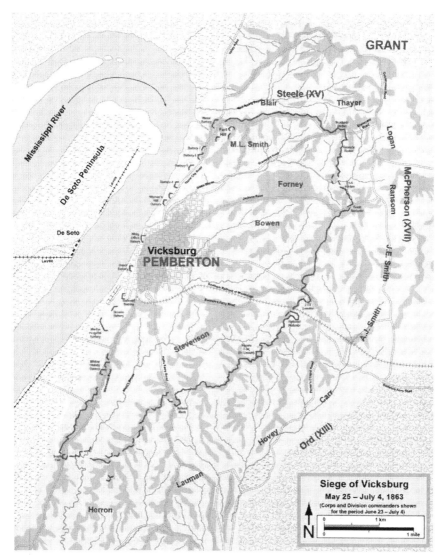

The final arrangement of troops during the Siege of Vicksburg from May 25th to July 4th, 1863. (Blue for Northerners, red for Southerners.)

Map by Hal Jespersen, https://www.posix.com/CW/, CC BY 3.0
<https://creativecommons.org/licenses/by/3.0>, via Wikimedia Commons
https://commons.wikimedia.org/wiki/File:VicksburgSiege.png

Inside the ramparts, the Rebel forces had abundant ammunition, but food and water were running extremely low for everybody. The Union dammed off the creeks running into Vicksburg, and the Mississippi River could not easily be accessed because of the Union presence along the shores abutting the waterfront. Within the Southern entrapment, domestic dogs and cats began disappearing, and mule meat replaced the soldiers' rations when beef ran out. Rats became a delicacy in a dish called "squirrel stew" for starving soldiers who were eventually rationed to one handful of peas and rice and a single cup of water per day. (It should be noted these rats could have been the local muskrat, indigenous to the wetlands of North America, which would have been eaten by many before wartime.) By the end of June, the price of dry goods had skyrocketed within Vicksburg, and the soldiers were showing signs of scurvy. Dysentery, cholera, and malaria further wasted the emaciated Confederate soldiers.

The internal press of Vicksburg (the *Vicksburg Daily Citizen*) continued reporting on the siege, as well as the living conditions within the town. When paper ran out, they used wallpaper to both write and print on. On July 2nd, two days before the town surrendered, Vicksburg's press was still boasting about winning the standoff. Its editor, J. W. Swords, wrote in response to Grant's supposition that he would be dining in Vicksburg by July 4th. "Ulysses must get into the city before he dines in it. The way to cook a rabbit is first to catch it."

But a note in the *Vicksburg Daily Citizen* at the end of the siege reads as follows:

July 4th, 1863: "Two days bring about great changes. The banner of the Union floats over Vicksburg. Gen. Grant has 'caught the rabbit;' he has dined in Vicksburg, and he did bring his dinner with him. The 'Citizen' lives to see it. For the last time it appears on 'Wall-paper.' No more will it eulogize the luxury of mule-meat and fricassed kitten— urge Southern warriors to such diet never more. This is the last wall-paper edition and is, excepting this note, from the types as we found them. It will be valuable hereafter as a curiosity."

This was the final insert of the *Vicksburg Daily Citizen*. The strange, ironic wording of the note is due to it having been engineered by the Union soldiers themselves. Upon entering Vicksburg on July 4th, they had found the printing tablet still laid out with the confident Confederate comments of July 2nd. The Northern soldiers took it upon themselves to rearrange the text, print fifty copies on the last remaining wallpaper, and sell them to fellow soldiers as keepsakes!

A photograph of the underground bombproof dugout dwellings in the yellow clay hills of the town during the Siege of Vicksburg, with the Shirley House (the "White House") in the background.

https://commons.wikimedia.org/wiki/File:ShirleysWhiteHouseVicksburg1863.jpg

During the siege, General Ulysses Grant kept a careful eye on General Johnston's movements near the Big Black River. Grant created a double line of entrenchments—one pointing toward Vicksburg and a second parallel but facing outward to guard against a Confederate encroachment from the land. He also reinforced his artillery by acquiring cannons from Union gunboats. However, Johnston was clearly reluctant to join the fight at Vicksburg and was more concerned with other Union activities around Mississippi. Northern reinforcements and troops continued to arrive at Vicksburg during the siege, and eventually, the Confederates within the town were outnumbered four to one.

The Union soldiers and sappers (quasi engineer soldiers employed to build bridges, dig trenches, and build abatis, etc.) busied themselves during the siege by continually extending and reinforcing their lines, tightening the noose around Vicksburg's neck and making it impossible for food and ordnance supplies to reach the town. They dug trenches toward the besieged town in zigzag patterns, hiding behind sap rollers to protect them as they worked. (Sap rollers were large cylinders of soft materials.) The zigzag trenches enabled the Federal soldiers to move ever closer to the ramparts of Vicksburg, with the erratic patterns making their movements more difficult to target by the Confederate sharpshooters above.

General Grant ordered mining operations below the ramparts, and on June 25th and July 1st, the Union exploded underground mines, with twenty hours of hand-to-hand combat continuing in the first instance in a four-meter (twelve-foot) deep crater. The 3rd Louisiana Redan on the Jackson Road leading east was severely damaged, and there were many Confederate casualties. The Northerners continued to burrow toward Vicksburg, and Pemberton's Confederates needed to countermine these efforts since they were infringed on many fronts by the digging activity. By the beginning of July, the Union had prepared a wide tunnel near the 3rd Louisiana Redan. It was large enough for a column of four men abreast to pass through, and rumors began sweeping through the Confederates that Grant would soon go on the offensive again. These efforts likely contributed to the surrender shortly thereafter.

During the siege, the Confederates continued forays to destabilize the Union, and one Rebel raid resulted in burning the ironclad *Cincinnati* warship that had already been considerably damaged on the Mississippi from Rebel artillery fire. (The ship was later salvaged and put back into Union service.) Confederate attempts to relieve Vicksburg from the western bank of the Mississippi in Louisiana continued throughout the siege. Confederate Major General John George Walker's Texas Division (known as "Walker's Greyhounds" for their speed and agility) had followed the Federals south in their pursuit of a river crossing that had ultimately been at Bruinsburg, but mismanagement by his subordinates saw the Yankees escape back into the Mississippi to continue with their campaign.

Walker led unsuccessful attacks west of the Mississippi on June 7th and July 4th, to no avail. The June assaults as Milliken's Bend and Young's Point saw savage fighting against untrained but highly motivated black troops from Mississippi and Louisiana. (Although the Union won this skirmish, they lost 652 men to the Confederates' 185.) Other encounters in Louisiana between the Blues and the Grays west of the Mississippi did not result in lasting success for the Southerners. In many instances, these encounters constituted enlisted black men protecting former slaves and newly acquired Union plantations or Union strongholds and supply depots. The final confrontation in early July at Helena, Arkansas, resulted in a disastrous defeat for the Rebels. As far as the Union was concerned, Vicksburg was safe from a river approach.

The siege that had begun in approximately mid-May of 1863 was proving too difficult for the Southerners to withstand. As July approached, General Pemberton needed to realistically abandon hope that help would come from the trans-Mississippi to the west or Johnston from the east. When he received a letter signed by "Many Soldiers" under his command that suggested surrender rather than their forced desertion, Pemberton had the good sense to begin planning a surrender. Both Generals Bowen and Martin Luther Smith advised against a breakout, citing an escape as impossible. Surrender was the only option available to the Southerners, and on July 3rd, two Confederate soldiers bearing a white flag finally rode out to the Union line. Negotiations for a surrender began.

Chapter 5 – Capturing the Mississippi River

At first, Union General Grant insisted upon unconditional surrender, as he had demanded at the Battle of Fort Donelson in February the year before. An unconditional surrender would require that all Rebel men, arms, and ordnances be turned over to the Yankees. Pemberton refused, threatening many more Union fatalities if Grant did not negotiate. With the assistance of generals on both sides, such as Bowen and Sherman, Grant and Pemberton finally agreed on terms. The Confederate soldiers were required to give up all battle arms, and they would be paroled rather than becoming prisoners of war. General Ulysses S. Grant correctly anticipated that sending the demoralized and emaciated Rebels home in shame would have more impact than capturing the men. Grant was convinced that the Union did not have the resources to care for tens of thousands of captives. The parolees were required to promise not to fight until such time as they were exchanged, a man for a man, for captured Federal prisoners being held by the Confederacy.

The official surrender was conducted near an oak tree on July 3rd in the afternoon, and although there are no photographs of the conversation, there are illustrations of the two generals meeting. In his memoirs, Grant described the fate of the poor tree, stating, "It was but a short time before the last vestige of its body root and limb had disappeared, the fragments taken as trophies." On July 4th—America's Independence Day—Grant and several divisions of his men marched into the surrendered town of Vicksburg, which they would permanently occupy for the remainder of the war. Despite having so recently been at each other's throats, Union soldiers reached out in extraordinary acts of humanity, providing their foes with food, water, and medical assistance.

As the Union flag of stars and stripes flew above Vicksburg, the dejected and angry Rebel soldiers were allowed to leave the town beginning on July 6th (it is not known how many days they needed to leave). After stacking their military weapons in immense piles (totaling seventy thousand rifles and muskets), furling their Confederate flags, and signing parole papers, they could make their way home. They were permitted to keep personal possessions, including sidearms and one horse per man. (Grant insisted that personal property was to specifically exclude slaves.) Many of the Rebel soldiers were inadvertently admitted back into the war by the following year against the agreement of the parole. Eventually, General Grant ceased all wartime exchanges and parole measures since the Confederates were not upholding their end of the bargain. The Confederate commanders captured after the siege were later exchanged for Union prisoners of similar rank, and Pemberton was returned to Richmond in mid-October of the same year.

Although records differ, the Siege of Vicksburg resulted in approximately three thousand Confederates killed, wounded, or missing, with the remainder of the Army of Mississippi (about twenty-seven thousand men) surrendering to the opposition. They were technically removed from the war unless they were later exchanged. Of these surrendered men, about two thousand were officers. During the siege, about eight hundred Northerners were killed, almost four thousand men were wounded, and two to three hundred were captured or went missing. Almost two hundred cannons were captured by the US in the siege alone, not counting those scooped up by Federal forces in the preliminary battles of the Vicksburg campaign. Sadly, an enormous number of horses (and one camel) were killed during the campaign, particularly those used to transport Confederate artillery. It was reported that the sheer volume of horse corpses around enemy batteries after the Battle of Champion Hill proved impossible for the Union to capture immediately.

During the Siege of Vicksburg, Confederate General Joseph E. Johnston had been gathering a force of thirty thousand men in Jackson. Johnston's intention was to relieve Pemberton and the town of Vicksburg from the siege, and he had been slowly encroaching on Vicksburg. However, Johnston tarried, complaining to Richmond (the Confederate headquarters in Virginia) that he did not have enough men. It was only by July 1st that the Jackson Confederates began inching their way west toward Vicksburg.

Communications between Pemberton and Johnston had always been poor. It was apparent that the generals rarely agreed and had continued to ignore each other's correspondence and requests throughout the campaign. It had also been extremely difficult for the Confederates to consult across the siege lines of Vicksburg and get messages in and out of the beleaguered town. At the time of the surrender, the Confederate troops from Jackson were positioned near the Big Black River. After Pemberton's capitulation, Johnston began marching his troops toward the Union's rear as they took command of Vicksburg.

On July 5th, Grant dispatched Sherman to confront Johnston, resulting in the Jackson Expedition, which was the final encounter of the Vicksburg campaign. Sherman's 9th, 15th, 13th, and part of the 16th Corps of the Army of the Tennessee chased Johnston's Confederate troops east over the Big Black River and farther beyond Champion Hill. This group of Southerners regrouped in Jackson. By July 10th, the Federal troops had surrounded Jackson and attacked two days later, albeit unsuccessfully. A standoff lasting from July 9th to July 17th ensued, as the Union surrounded the western extremities of the town in a semicircular arc reaching from north to south. This is known as the Siege of Jackson.

Johnston chose to evacuate the state capital for the second time in the Vicksburg campaign and removed his men by July 16th, abandoning the town to the Yankees. Jackson came under Federal command once again, which was yet another coup for the Northerners, who had spent 1862 and 1863 bagging strategic nodes in the Western Theater. The Siege of Jackson safeguarded Federal control over Vicksburg and officially ended the Vicksburg campaign. The completion of Sherman's Jackson Expedition was one of the highlights of his career, as it ensured that the Mississippi River remained in Union hands for the remainder of the war.

Simultaneous to the Siege of Vicksburg, the battle for Port Hudson in eastern Louisiana, 241 kilometers (about 150 miles) south downriver of Vicksburg, had continued from May 22nd to July 9th, 1863. Port Hudson lay just 32 kilometers (20 miles) north of Baton Rouge and 161 kilometers (100 miles) upriver from New Orleans—the closest major southern town before the Gulf of Mexico and the open ocean. Union General Nathaniel Prentice Banks (1816-1894, a politician who served in the Civil War) was tasked with overrunning Port Hudson before heading north to assist Grant with the Siege of Vicksburg. However, after several unsuccessful attacks on the fort, General Banks was forced to lay siege to Port Hudson for forty-eight days (one day longer than the Siege of Vicksburg). It was the longest siege in US military history at that time. (Banks's 19th Corps included black soldiers from Louisiana who were part of two desperate but failed assaults on Port Hudson on May 27th and June 11th.)

Five days after the surrender at the Siege of Vicksburg, Confederate General Franklin Kitchell Gardner (1823-1873, a career military man who served the Confederacy for the Civil War and has been heralded for his heroic stand during the siege) finally surrendered Port Hudson. Beginning on July 9ᵗʰ, 1863, the Union controlled the entire Mississippi, from its mouth at the gulf all the way north upstream into Northern territory, including all the major tributaries. It was a defining moment in the war. The Rebels would not regain this prized lost ground or the strategic nodes along the mighty Mississippi. The river that divided the western from the eastern Southern territories was now a major supply line for their adversaries.

Most of the Confederates who fought for Port Hudson were similarly paroled as those at Vicksburg. Approximately nine thousand Union soldiers were casualties of death, injury, disease, or severe sunstroke after the Siege of Port Hudson. Only approximately nine hundred men on Gardner's side were injured, dead, or incapacitated. General Banks kindly provided transport to the sick and diseased Confederate soldiers, returning home with extremely sick men who remained under the care of the Union. Almost six thousand Southern soldiers and civilians were paroled after this final Mississippi coup, with about four hundred men being imprisoned. By September of 1863, most of the parolees from Port Hudson had returned to duty, much to the fury of some Northern commanders. However, it was agreed on both sides that the terms of the parole had been unsubstantiated.

Chapter 6 – Outcome of the Vicksburg Campaign

Within these first few years of the Civil War, many Confederate successes in the Eastern Theater were attributed to poor appointments at the head of the Northern Army, the subsequent degeneration of communication between generals, and even insubordination. At the same time, in the Western Theater, in which the Siege of Vicksburg had transpired, incoherent communication and orders between the Southern leaders had been a significant contributing factor to the loss of Vicksburg and, as a result, the control of the Mississippi. General Pemberton showed consistent indecisiveness and hesitation as he attempted to please two masters: President Davis, who'd insisted that he hold Vicksburg at all costs, and General Johnston, who was attempting to make immediate tactical decisions in the heat of the campaign.

Pemberton's hesitation in following Johnston's orders during the Battle of Champion Hill could have potentially fed Johnston's reluctance to attack the Union's rear during the Siege of Vicksburg. It was apparent that Johnston made no real effort to relieve General Pemberton, his army, or the town of Vicksburg itself. After the fall of Vicksburg, fingers were pointed in all directions, and General John

Pemberton demanded a court inquiry into General Johnston's delay in sending aid to Vicksburg, but a court-martial was never ordered.

The Union's success at the Siege of Vicksburg resulted in its domination of the Mississippi River, the crucially strategic arterial route through the Southern war theaters. The piece of river referred to as "Gibraltar" that had been under Confederate control systematically gave way to Union forces soon after the siege. The section that stretched from Vicksburg to Port Hudson was the main thoroughfare for food, men, and supplies from the western to the eastern states of the Southern territories. Blocking the easy flow of goods, particularly the products of agriculture grown in the trans-Mississippi, essentially cleaved the South in two. The conclusion of the Siege of Vicksburg was a dramatic and final turning point in the Civil War that saw the gradual demise of the Rebels. Coupled with the Union victory at Gettysburg the day before on July 3rd, 1863, in Northern territory (Pennsylvania), the war had turned in favor of the Federals, but it would take a further two years for the North to finally crush the indomitable South.

General John Pemberton was demoted in 1864, but he continued serving the war to its close in the Eastern Theater, albeit in unobtrusive roles. General Johnston assumed leadership of the Confederate Army of Tennessee in 1864 but was subsequently removed by President Davis during the Atlanta campaign (the summer of 1864, Western Theater). The truly outstanding Confederate individual from the Vicksburg campaign was General Bowen, who unfortunately died of dysentery shortly after the siege. He is considered as one of the greatest unsung Confederate heroes of the war, and he was accompanied everywhere by his wife, who refused to leave his side for the duration of the war.

For General Ulysses S. Grant, the Siege of Vicksburg paved the way for a glittering career and his immediate promotion to major general of the Regular Army (seasoned US soldiers). He was heralded as a national hero, and further wins in the Western Theater thereafter led to his appointment as the commanding general of the Union Army, an office he held from March 1864 until after the end of the Civil War in March of 1869. Confederate General-in-Chief Robert Edward Lee (1807–1870, a distinguished military soldier and engineer who commanded the Confederates for much of the Civil War) was required to make the final Southern surrender to Grant at Appomattox, Virginia, on April 9th, 1865, thus ending the Civil War. From 1869 to 1877, Ulysses S. Grant sat as the eighteenth president of the United States. Although several scandals tarnished his time in office, he was heralded as a symbol of national unity upon his death, and he has since been recognized for his considerable accomplishments, particularly with respect to civil, African American, and Native American rights and liberties.

General William T. Sherman's career was similarly made by the success of the Siege of Vicksburg, and he was appointed head of the Union Army in the Western Theater in 1864 once Grant was promoted. Sherman went on to enjoy military successes until the close of the war, and he succeeded Grant as the commander of the US Army, which he held for an astounding fourteen years until his retirement in 1883.

The Union's success at the Siege of Vicksburg is considered to be the most pivotal event in the Civil War. Capturing Vicksburg created a domino effect in which the last remaining piece of the Mississippi came under Union control. Once the Union held this mighty river that divided the country, they had fractured the South. Besides the militaristic and moral victory of Vicksburg, the Rebels could no longer use the north-south-running Mississippi nor the west-east-aligned Southern Railway to move men, supplies, and crucial communications to the battlefields east of the river. The North had broken the backbone of the South.

Unbeknownst to all who fought, the Civil War was at its midpoint. A further two years of fighting would finally see the crippled South capitulate. The Siege of Vicksburg had resulted in the disbanding of an entire Confederate Army—the Army of Mississippi. Now, only one army stood in the way of Union victory in the Western Theater: the Army of Tennessee.

Conclusion

The Siege of Vicksburg was arguably the most decisive battle of the American Civil War in that it swung the momentum of victory away from the South and toward the North. When the Union captured Vicksburg, they created insurmountable strategic and tactical difficulties for the Confederate forces. The Union success at Vicksburg and the resultant domination of the Mississippi meant that the cannons at Vicksburg remained silent for the remainder of the war—the town did not need to defend itself again, as it was permanently beaten. The Vicksburg campaign is described in US Army manuals as the most brilliant campaign ever waged on American soil and marks General Grant as the first amongst modern war tacticians.

Both presidents of the North and South had openly declared the strategic imperative of controlling Vicksburg. It was the crucial node on the eastern bank of the Mississippi that linked the Southern Railway that enabled the movement of troops, food, and supplies from Southern territories to the west of the Mississippi to the main battlefields east of the river. The high bluffs along the eastern bank of this mighty river meant that whoever controlled the towns on the high ground controlled the riverways, with the bluffs making for ideal artillery platforms aimed at the water.

In the winter of 1862, the race for Vicksburg began with the start of the Vicksburg campaign, which was initiated by General Ulysses S. Grant, who was both respected and chastised for his brilliance, bravery, and eccentricities. Grant was a master of diversionary tactics, and he ultimately chose the least likely strategy for gaining Vicksburg by sending tens of thousands of troops down the western side of the Mississippi, deep into enemy territory and knee-deep in mud, alligators, and deadly snakes. This sneak attack was considered so outlandish by the enemy that General Pemberton, who was in charge of protecting Vicksburg, did not believe it possible until it was too late.

The Confederates fought bravely for the first two weeks of May 1863 to prevent the Federals from reaching Vicksburg, but eventually, Pemberton and his men were forced behind the ramparts of the fortress-like town. For a further six weeks, the Rebels held firm, repelling the Union with all their might, and they never did manage to breach the fortifications. General Grant chose to starve and dig his enemy out, and they were finally willing to meet for negotiations to surrender on July 3rd. The Northern win at the Battle of Gettysburg on the same day may have contributed to General Pemberton's final decision to surrender.

Vicksburg saw the removal of an entire army from the Confederacy. One could see the visibly diminished morale of Southern troops as they piled their weapons on a heap with tears in their eyes before returning to their homes, no longer permitted to continue as Southern soldiers. In the words of President Abraham Lincoln, "[the Mississippi again rolled] unvexed to the sea," unaware that its loss was symbolic of the South's failure to rise again. The Rebel spine had been broken, and the Southern lands to the west of the river lay immobile, as they were unable to provide the support that the theater to the east would so desperately need in the years to come.

Here's another book by Captivating History that you might like

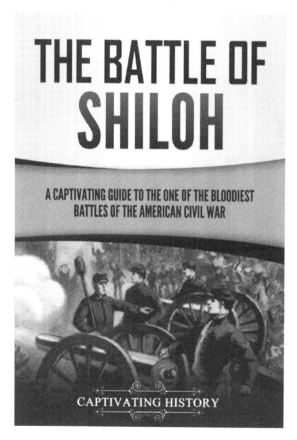

Free Bonus from Captivating History
(Available for a Limited time)

Hi History Lovers!

Now you have a chance to join our exclusive history list so you can get your first history ebook for free as well as discounts and a potential to get more history books for free! Simply visit the link below to join.

Captivatinghistory.com/ebook

Also, make sure to follow us on Facebook, Twitter and Youtube by searching for Captivating History.

References

American Battlefield Trust:

Vicksburg, https://www.battlefields.org/learn/civil-war/battles/vicksburg, accessed July, August 2021,

: *Vicksburg: Animated Battle Map*, YouTube video, https://www.youtube.com/watch?v=1eSgimZ8GKQ, accessed July, August 2021.

Britannica.com:
Vicksburg Campaign, https://www.britannica.com/event/Vicksburg-Campaign, accessed July, August 2021.

DePue, Dr. Mark, 2015. Abraham Lincoln Presidential Library and Museum. YouTube Video, *The Civil War Battle Series: Vicksburg*, https://www.youtube.com/watch?v=hyTVOPTTa6k, accessed July, August 2021.

History.com:
Grant: Massive Siege of Vicksburg Leads to Union Victory, YouTube video, https://www.youtube.com/watch?v=qnq-df4MQzI, accessed July, August 2021.

Mann, Meredith, June 30, 2016. *The Writing on the Wall: Documenting Civil War History*, New York Public Library,

Manuscripts and Archives Division, Stephen A. Schwarzman
Building, https://www.nypl.org/blog/2016/06/30/vicksburg-daily-
citizen, July, August 2021.

National Park Service:

Civil War Series 24, Section 1-9,

https://www.nps.gov/parkhistory/online_books/civil_war_series/24/sec
1.htm, July,

August 2021,

Here Brothers Fought, The Siege of Vicksburg, The Official NPS
Theater Film, https://www.nps.gov/vick/index.htm, July, August 2021.

Ohio History Central:

Siege of Vicksburg,
https://ohiohistorycentral.org/w/Siege_of_Vicksburg, accessed July,
August 2021.

U.S. Army Heritage & Education Center:

Siege of Vicksburg,

https://ahec.armywarcollege.edu/exhibits/CivilWarImagery/cheney_vi
cksburg.cfm, accessed July, August 2021.

Wikipedia.com:
Battle of Champion Hill,
https://en.wikipedia.org/wiki/Battle_of_Champion_Hill, accessed July,
August 2021

Confederate States of America,

https://en.wikipedia.org/wiki/Confederate_States_of_America,
accessed July, August 2021,

John S. Bowen,
https://en.wikipedia.org/wiki/John_S._Bowen#American_Civil_War,
accessed July, August 2021,

John C. Pemberton,
https://en.wikipedia.org/wiki/John_C._Pemberton#Vicksburg,
accessed July, August 2021,

Siege of Port Hudson,
https://en.wikipedia.org/wiki/Siege_of_Port_Hudson, accessed July,
August 2021,

Siege of Vicksburg, https://en.wikipedia.org/wiki/Siege_of_Vicksburg,
accessed July, August 2021,

Ulysses S. Grant, https://en.wikipedia.org/wiki/Ulysses_S._Grant,
accessed July, August 2021,

Vicksburg Campaign,
https://en.wikipedia.org/wiki/Vicksburg_campaign, accessed July,
August 2021,

Vicksburg, Mississippi,
https://en.wikipedia.org/wiki/Vicksburg,_Mississippi, accessed July,
August 2021,

Western Theater of the American Civil War,

https://en.wikipedia.org/wiki/Western_Theater_of_the_American_Ci
vil_War, accessed July, August 2021,

William Tecumseh Sherman,

https://en.wikipedia.org/wiki/William_Tecumseh_Sherman#Vicksbur
g, accessed July, August 2021.

Made in the USA
Las Vegas, NV
01 November 2023

80078735R00042